Backyard Bugs

Flying Colors

Butterflies in Your Backyard

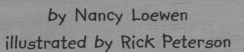

by Nancy Loewen

illustrated by Rick Peterson

Thanks to our advisers for their expertise, research, knowledge, and advice:

Blake Newton, Extension Entomologist
University of Kentucky

Susan Kesselring, M.A., Literacy Educator
Rosemount–Apple Valley–Eagan (Minnesota) School District

PICTURE WINDOW BOOKS
Minneapolis, Minnesota

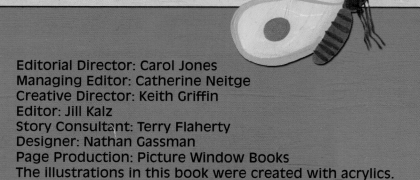

Editorial Director: Carol Jones
Managing Editor: Catherine Neitge
Creative Director: Keith Griffin
Editor: Jill Kalz
Story Consultant: Terry Flaherty
Designer: Nathan Gassman
Page Production: Picture Window Books
The illustrations in this book were created with acrylics.

Picture Window Books
5115 Excelsior Boulevard
Suite 232
Minneapolis, MN 55416
877-845-8392
www.picturewindowbooks.com

Printed in the United States of America.

Library of Congress Cataloging-in-Publication Data
Loewen, Nancy, 1964–
Flying colors : butterflies in your backyard / by Nancy Loewen ; illustrated by
Rick Peterson.
p. cm. — (Backyard bugs)
ISBN 1-4048-1143-5 (hardcover)
1. Butterflies—Juvenile literature. I. Peterson, Rick, ill. II. Title.
QL544.2.L669 2005
595.78'9—dc22
                                                        2005004059

Table of Contents

Flying Colors

They're orange, yellow, red, blue, brown, and black. They're striped, spotted, and swirled.

See how they flit over the flowers?
What are these colorful dancers?

Butterflies!

A Flower's Friend

Go ahead, get closer.
Do you see the butterfly
crawling on the flower?
It's tasting the flower
with the special hairs
on its feet.

6

That flower must taste good because now the butterfly is eating. It has unwound its mouthpart and is drinking a sweet liquid called nectar from the flower.

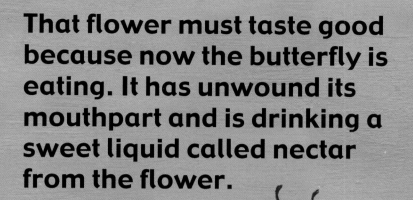

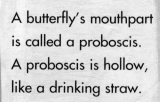

A butterfly's mouthpart is called a proboscis. A proboscis is hollow, like a drinking straw.

Butterflies don't hurt flowers by drinking their nectar. In fact, butterflies are very helpful. They help the plants make more plants.

Inside a flower is a powder called pollen. Plants need pollen from other plants to grow seeds and fruit. When a butterfly lands on a flower, bits of pollen stick to its legs. The butterfly then spreads this pollen from flower to flower. Spreading pollen is called pollination.

A butterfly chooses flowers based on the length of its proboscis. The nectar in some flowers is deep inside, and only a butterfly with a long proboscis can reach it.

9

Winging It

Have you ever caught a butterfly by its wings? Did some powder come off on your fingers? That powder is actually made of tiny scales.

A butterfly needs these scales like a bird needs feathers. The scales help a butterfly fly and keep its body at the right temperature.

So, if you want to catch a butterfly, the best way is to use a net. Try not to touch the butterfly's wings. And be sure to let it go when you're done looking at it.

Butterflies have two large wings and two smaller ones. The wings are made of very thin layers of skin with a bunch of veins in between.

A Special Dance

Look! Up there! Two butterflies are fluttering around each other. They are a male and a female doing a special dance. Soon they will mate, and the female will lay eggs on the leaves of a plant.

Butterflies have smelling parts on their antennae that help them find other butterflies with which to mate.

13

From Caterpillar to Chrysalis

When a butterfly egg hatches, what do you think will come out? A tiny butterfly? Not at all. A tiny caterpillar! It eats leaves and grows. It sheds its skin four or five times before it is done growing.

A butterfly's life cycle is divided into four parts: egg, larva, pupa, and adult. The caterpillar is the larva.

One day, the caterpillar starts to change.
With its mouth, it spins a patch of silk onto
a branch or leaf. Then it attaches itself to the
silk and hangs upside down. It sheds its outer skin one
last time, displaying a hard outer shell called a chrysalis.
The butterfly is now called a pupa.

Some kinds of pupae stay in their chrysalises for only a week. Some stay for several years.

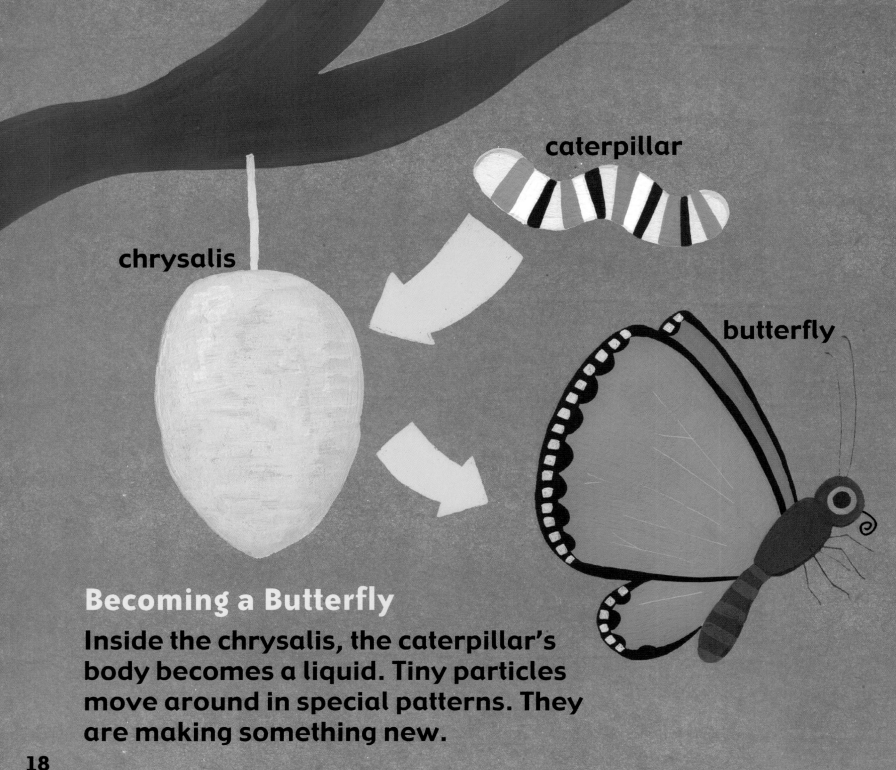

caterpillar

chrysalis

butterfly

Becoming a Butterfly

Inside the chrysalis, the caterpillar's body becomes a liquid. Tiny particles move around in special patterns. They are making something new.

Finally, the chrysalis
hatches—and yes,
here is the butterfly!

When a butterfly comes
out of its chrysalis, its
wings are crumpled
and wet. The butterfly
has to wait for its wings
to dry before it can fly.

There it goes, off to find some flowers!

Look Closely at a Butterfly

Look at a butterfly through a magnifying glass. How many of these different parts can you see?

- A butterfly uses its **antennae** to touch and smell.
- Each **eye** sees well close-up but not far away.
- A butterfly drinks through its straw-like **proboscis**.
- The six **legs** are jointed, or able to bend.
- A butterfly holds up its two **fore wings** and two **hind wings** when it's resting.

antennae

fore wing

eye

proboscis

hind wing

legs

head

thorax

abdomen

Fun Facts

- Butterflies can be found in forests, grasslands, deserts, and mountains—everywhere except in Antarctica.

- In some kinds of butterflies, males and females look exactly the same to the human eye—but there are hidden patterns that only the butterflies can see.

- The world's smallest butterfly is the blue pygmy, found in southern California. When its wings are open, it measures 1.5 inches (3.8 centimeters) from the tip of one fore wing to the tip of the other. The largest butterfly, Queen Alexandra's Birdwing, is found in New Guinea. It measures up to 12 inches (30.5 centimeters) from wing tip to wing tip.

A Chrysalis Craft

You've probably made a lot of butterflies at school and at home. But have you ever made a chrysalis?

Get an empty toilet paper tube. Flatten one end slightly and have an adult help you cut it into a rounded shape. Glue or staple this end shut. (Be sure to ask for help when stapling, if you need it.)

Now for the fun part—decorating! Use markers, paint, glitter, beads, scraps of wrapping paper—anything you like. When your chrysalis is dry, cut the tip off an old sock and put it over the open end of the tube. Secure it with a rubber band. You can slip an ornament hook or a paper clip into the sock if you want to hang up your chrysalis.

But your chrysalis is still missing something, isn't it? Cut a butterfly out of paper, fold it up, and slip it into the tube.

When do you think it will hatch?

Words to Know

antennae – Antennae (an-TEN-ee) are feelers on a bug's head. They are used for touching and smelling. Antennae is the word for more than one antenna (an-TEN-uh).

chrysalis – A chrysalis (KRI-seh-les) is the shell in which a caterpillar changes into a butterfly.

larva – A newly hatched butterfly is called a larva. It looks like a worm.

mate – Male and female butterflies mate by joining together special parts of their bodies. After they've mated, the female butterfly can lay eggs.

proboscis – A proboscis (preh-BAH-ses) is a long, hollow mouthpart. A butterfly uses its proboscis to drink nectar.

pupa – When a butterfly is changing from a larva to an adult, it is called a pupa (PYOO-puh). Pupae (PYOO-pee) is the word for more than one pupa.

scales – Scales are hard, overlapping parts on the wings of certain bugs, such as moths, butterflies, and mosquitoes.

veins – Veins are thin tubes that help give shape to a bug's wings.

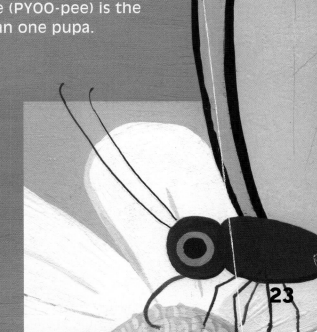

To Learn More

At the Library

Muther, Connie. *My Monarch Journal*. Nevada City, Calif.: Dawn Publications, 2000.

Wallace, Karen. *Born to Be a Butterfly*. New York: Dorling Kindersley Publishing, 2000.

White, Nancy. *Butterfly Battle*. New York: Scholastic, 2003.

On the Web

FactHound offers a safe, fun way to find Web sites related to this book. All of the sites on FactHound have been researched by our staff. *www.facthound.com*

1. Visit the FactHound home page.
2. Enter a search word related to this book, or type in this special code: 1404811435.
3. Click on the FETCH IT button.

Your trusty FactHound will fetch the best sites for you!

Look for all of the books in the Backyard Bugs series:

Busy Buzzers: Bees in Your Backyard

Bzzz, Bzzz! Mosquitoes in Your Backyard

Chirp, Chirp! Crickets in Your Backyard

Dancing Dragons: Dragonflies in Your Backyard

Flying Colors: Butterflies in Your Backyard

Garden Wigglers: Earthworms in Your Backyard

Hungry Hoppers: Grasshoppers in Your Backyard

Living Lights: Fireflies in Your Backyard

Night Fliers: Moths in Your Backyard

Spotted Beetles: Ladybugs in Your Backyard

Tiny Workers: Ants in Your Backyard

Weaving Wonders: Spiders in Your Backyard